Secrets of the Qur'an

Paytah Zeke

authorHOUSE®

AuthorHouse™
1663 Liberty Drive
Bloomington, IN 47403
www.authorhouse.com
Phone: 1-800-839-8640

First published by AuthorHouse 8/5/2009

ISBN: 978-1-4389-8947-1 (sc)

Printed in the United States of America
Bloomington, Indiana

This book is printed on acid-free paper.

The Islamic Religion known as the Muslims are the ONLY People who believe that their god "Allah" must rule over the world, and this comes from the Muslims messengers who are given commands from Allah, and are handed down to the Muslim people to carry out.

Islam is a very dangerous and serious religion, all through the Qur'an talks about killing people who do not accept Allah as their god, Or demands their life.

Because Satan hates people who follow the Supreme God and His Divine Trinity, called the Father, Son and Holy Spirit, Then Satan "or Allah" commands any non believer to be slain, he brings his message to the people through a book called the Qur'an and some verses are in this book for your information.

This book will give view points on what the Qur'an is about in theory and fact, I will use the translation given by A. Yusuf Ali, 1934, and I will use the King James Version Bible, copyright 1981, to demonstrate many items of interest.

Not the spelling variations differ on Arabic key words, the Islamic prophet known as Mohammed, Mohammad, Mohamued and Muhammad, and the Islam spelling of the Coran, Koran, Qo'ran, Quron, and Qur'an. I will use the spelling of Mohammad and Qur'an for the given information.

I will earnestly establish the falsehood and gross misconception of how the Qur'an has brought false teaching to Millions and Millions of people who call themselves, "Islamic Muslims".

The definition of a religion Cult. Is a religion who does not recognize "Jesus Christ" as Lord and Savior and removes His Deity in any way, and adding or taking away from His Holy Word, The Bible.

The Islamic Religion is just ONE of many religions that are known as a Cult religion. The English translations of the Qur'an, numbering of the verses differs from one translation to another, this is why I have specifically given notice that I will use A. Yusuf Ali's translation over Abdullah Yusuf Ali's translation of the Qur'an.

First I will explain who or what "Allah" is.. Allah is a god of the Islamic Book called the Qur'an, Sometimes you will hear Muslims call the Qur'an their bible, most people will assume that the Christian Bible God and the god of the Qur'an are one and the same, but just different names, "This is totally False" Comparing the attributes of Allah found in the Qur'an and the attributes in the Bible, is like night and day, or white and black.

The god "Allah" was known to the Arabs thousands of years before Mohammad, the founder of the Qur'an, supposedly handed down from Allah, see Sura 47: 2, which states, Those who believe and work deeds of righteousness, and believe in the (Revelation) sent down to Muhammad, for it is the truth from their Lord. And Sura 59: 21, states, Had we sent down this Qur'an on a mountain, verily, thou would have seen it humble itself and cleave asunder for fear of Allah.

Looking into the Encyclopedia Britannica gives Arabic inscriptions to Allah prior to the religion "Islam".

Mohammad was born within the tribe of Quraysh which was Arabic in the year 570 A.D. in Mecca, and was devoted to "Allah" the moon god. It is easy to see that Allah is the moon god for Muslims, they use the crescent of the moon on their flag and most other symbols they use for show.

In reading the Qur'an, it is clear that a lot of it's history, ideas and writings came from the Bible, in the most twisted way known to man it is also clear that the Qur'an was written to destroy the Bible teachings in every way possible. As God is the Author and ONLY instrument through man, who gave us "NO Private interpretation in the Bible" see 2 Peter 1: 20. KJV.

From what I see, Satan is the author, who is the one of the Antichrist's and instrument, through man who has written the Qur'an. It is noted that the opening letter of A. Yusuf Ali. He does his best to explain his English interpretation, he said, side by side with the Arabic text "not one word from another" but his full expression. He wants to make the Islamic language "English" and if anyone has any criticism of the Qur'an, he would like to hear from them, he also explains that he has taken the liberty to use many other ideas and collected books, materials and has taken notes from societies and included the thoughts and hearts of the western world. This is clearly a message that, he simply used the bible to twist the words from the bible to his Qur'an.

Why would any one who is making a translation from Arabic to English want to seek out notes and opinions of others, who have bias theories, this obviously cannot be a true translation, but then when you starts with some things made up, you end up with the same.

Sura 27: 64 states in part, can there be another god besides "Allah" ? (Say, bring forth your argument if you are telling the truth.) There are many false gods, but only one True God, who is God the Father of Heaven and Earth. And it is well known that only His children will know Him, see 2 Corinthians 4: 3 and 4. Quote, "If the Gospel be hid, it is hid to them that are lost: in whom the god of this world, (Satan) hath blinded the minds of them which believe not, lest the light of the Glorious Gospel of Christ Jesus who is the Image of God, should shine unto them. Unquote, let me add, that God the Father knows us before we are born, and He would not give salvation to anyone knowing that they would trash it later.

All through the Qur'an you will note that Allah is male, just bringing up one for reference, Sura 5: 17 states, "If Allah touch thee with afflictions, none can remove it be he".. When I talked with many Muslims, they say Allah is not a male or female, this is what they are told and not what they read, only because Christians call God, the Father, which makes Him a Male, Muslims denounce God being male immediately, only because of the Christians following the Father God.

The Qur'an states many places that "god is more than one", the Qur'an will talk about Allah as "we or us" which clearly shows that more then one is being explained. See Sura 15: 23, It is "we" who gave life and who gave death.
Sura 16: 40 "We" say "be" and it is.

Muslims will vehemently denounce that the "Trinity" exists, the Bible show many places that the Trinity in the God Head is Real. However some Cult religions will denounce His "Three in One" concept as reality.

Sura 2: 7 states, In the Qur'an, Allah has put a veil on nonbelievers eyes, not to see, and has sealed their hearts and ears, then has given non-believers chastisement.

Jesus explained in John 12: 40 – 50 In part, If any man hear my Words and believe not, I judge him not; I come not to judge the world, but to save the world, if you believe in Me.

Sura 2: 29 states that he, Allah hath created for you all the things that are on earth, "then" he turned to heaven and made them into seven firmaments (heavens). This statement is erratic and backwards, what it is saying is the earth is not in any of the heavens, and after earth comes seven heavens, See Sura 71: 15 and 78: 12 (See how Allah as created the seven heavens one above another.)

2 Cor. 12: 2 is clear, "Three Heavens" is what we have, Our earth and sky is one, our Stars and planets are in the second, and God's abode is the Third.

It is very interesting how Satan cannot deny the fact that God will (and has) sent His Only Begotten Son, Jesus Christ to earth to preach and shed His Blood for ALL Sinners who believe in Him

Sura 2: 30 states, Allah said to the angles, I will create a vicegerent "Deputy of a King" on earth, "Meaning Jesus Christ" and the angles asked, wilt thou place there in one who will make mischief, "with the Jews?" And shed Blood "His Blood"? And the angles will celebrate the praises and glorify thy Holy Name ! "Jesus Christ".

Sura 2: 34. 7: 11, 61 18: 50. 20: 16 and 28: 72 ALL state "We" said to the angles, "Bow down to Adam" However this is not understood and confusing with the Muslims, as Jesus is the "Second Adam" see 1 Cor. 15: 45 & 47, State, the first Adam was made a living Soul; the LAST ADAM, was made a quickening Spirit.

The First man is of the earth, earthy: the Second man is the Lord from Heaven.

Sura 2: 25 states, give glad tidings to those who believe and "Work Righteousness", that their portion is ""Gardens beneath which rivers flow there from " They say, "Why" this is what we were fed with before, for they are given things in similitude, and they have their in spouses purified, and they abide there forever. It is obvious that Muslims will be in a place with many virgins, but where the virgins come from is a Mystery.
So they do believe that they must earn their way to bliss, which is gardens with rivers, see Sura's 3: 15, 136 4: 13, 57, 122. 5: 12, 85, 119. And 9: 72, 89, 100.

As it looks like some Muslims have read the bible and copied wording, as reported in Sura 2: 34 and many more like these verses, having the angles bow down to Adam could be only understood as the "Second Adam" who is Jesus Himself.. Moreover, heaven is not gardens with rivers and women, in the Bible, Mark 12: 25 is clear, Marriage is not possible in heaven, and working for bliss is not possible, as states in Eph. 2: 8, 9. For by Grace are you saved through Faith, and that Not of yourselves, it is a gift of God, NOT of works, lease any man should boast.

Clearly, Ishmael, is the seed of the Islam who have "No Covenant" or Promise with God, as stated in Gen. 17: 19 in part. " I will establish My covenant with him " ISAAC" for an EVERLASTING COVENANT, and with his SEED, "Not Seeds" after him .

How interesting in the Qur'an, Sura 5: 20 Talks about Moses who is giving his people instructions, and we all know that Moses was the leader of the Jewish people, but in the Qur'an, it tries hard to show Muslims were the people of Moses, of which the Muslims tribes did not exist as Muslims.

Also in Sur 5: 21 Moses says " enter the holy land which Allah hath assigned unto you, the holy land, being Israel of course, which was given to the Jews, How ironic the Muslims Think they have rights (today) to what Moses and God done thousands of years before Islam come together

How odd in Sura 5: 38, 39 any thief caught, the "hands must be cut off" for punishment from Allah, but wait,,, it gets better, If they repent after the crime,, Allah will return with forgiveness most merciful,, (But forget your hands.)

Sura 2: 40 states, O children of Israel ! Call to mind the "Special" favor which I bestowed upon you and fulfil your covenant with me and I shall fulfil my covenant with you and fear none but me.

Sura 2: 47 states, O children of Israel ! Call to mind the "Special" favor which I bestowed upon you that, "I preferred you to all others"

as you can see, the Qur'an is trying to show that the Christian God, " God the Father" is the god of the Muslims being Allah, in the Bible, it is clear who the Children are, God was speaking to Noah in Genesis 6: 13, 18 "God was ending all flesh with the exception of Noah and his wife, with three sons and their wives, a total of eight people.

Sura 37: 83 states,, "Abraham was in the Ark with Noah. The fact is, Abraham wasn't even born yet. Abraham appears after Noah, see Gen. 11: 27 and the Covenant was given to Abraham and his son Isaac, the First Jews, "the Children of Israel"

Sura 6: 74 state that Azar was Abraham's father, when the Bible documents "Terah" begat Abram with God changed to Abraham, see Gen. 17: 5. And at this time, God Blessed Abraham with His Covenant. God forwarded His promise with Noah in Gen 6: 18,

Noah and his family being eight members in total were saved from the earth flood, see Gen. 7: 1, 7, 13. Yet the Qur'an states that one of the sons of Noah refused to go into the Ark and was drowned in the flood. See Sura 11: 43. And it also claims that the Ark came to rest on top of Mount Judi which the bible states in Gen. 8: 4. It came to rest on Mount Ararat. There is some evidence of this from aerial photos during WW2.

As for the covenant of "Promise" Genesis 17: 7 states, God will make a covenant between God and Abraham. "Between Me and thee and they SEED after thee is their generations for an everlasting covenant" Notice that God did not say after they "seeds" but only One Seed. Also Gen. 17: 20 as for Ishmael, God had blessed him and will make him fruitful and will multiply him exceedingly, and will make him a great nation, which is true today in the Muslim world, But No Promise toward a Covenant of salvation.

Ishmael is the "Very Seed" that started Islam as a blessing with out promise, because he is from the bond women Hagar, the Egyptian. God heard her affliction with Sarai who is Abrahams wife, and God said her son "Ishmael" the son of Hagar will be a "Wild Man" and his hand will be "against every man, and every man against him," and he shall dwelling the presence of all his brethren, (which is in effect today and forever).

See Gen. 16: 12 this scripture is also backed up in Galatians 4: 28, 29. Which states now we brethren as Isaac was, are the Children of Promise "covenant" but as then he that was born after the flesh persecuted him " any Christian or Jew" that was born after the Spirit, even so it is now today.

Gal. 4: 30 is clear, the Bible scripture states, "for the son Ishmael" of the bond woman Hagar, shall be NOT the heir (covenant of God) with the son of the free women "Sarai" who is Isaac.

Sura 2: 65 and 7: 166 states that who ever transgressed the Sabbath, "we" said to them, "be ye Apes". Anyone knows that humans flesh cannot turn into animal, and it is not biblical that any human was ever an animal, this kind of action would not be reasonable or feasible to a true God. And at the same time, Sura 7: 167 states that the god of the Qur'an is forgiving and merciful. I would believe it all depends on if your talking about the One and only True God, or a false god.

Sura 2: 87 states "we" Gave Moses the book and followed him up with a succession of messengers. "We" gave Jesus the son of Mary clear "signs" and strengthened Him with the Holy Spirit. This statement is true when you read the bible,, as Jesus was strengthened by the Holy Spirit, simply put, the Trinity is One God in Three Divine Persons the bible clearly displays the Trinity although the Bible, although the Word Trinity is not in the Bible, "Three in One simply put, is a Trinity".

Sura 2: 113 states Jews and Christians are at odds against one another, as they study the same book, Actually the Orthodox Jews hold to the Old Testament, while the Christians hold to the Old and New Testament. But the Muslims have not been given this knowledge.

Sura 2: 116 states that "they say" Allah hath begotten a son,, but it is not to be believed my Muslims. And I say that is good because Allah being a false god cannot begot anything.

In the Bible, see 1 John 5: 7 and 8 Also 2 Cor. 13: 14 and Matthew 28: 19 Represents the Trinity at large, three in one …

Oddly enough Sura 2: 122 states "O children of Israel" Call to mind the special favor which I bestowed upon you. And that I "Allah" preferred you to all others, this would be taken from Gen. 17: 19 being a covenant of everlasting for the children of Israel.

Sura 2: 133 is falsified, the God of Abraham, "Ishmael" and "Isaac" Ishmael was not covered under God the Father with His Promise.

It is interesting this verse in Sura 2: 133 does say and I quote (Were you witnesses when death appeared before Jacob? Behold, he said to his sons, what will you worship after me? They said, We shall worship thy God and the God of they fathers, of Abraham, Ishmael and Isaac, The One True God do we submit.

Matthew 22: 32 and Mark 12: 26 state,,, I am the God of Abraham, the God of Isaac and the God of Jacob.

Sura 2: 144 and 149. Explains where the Muslims can receive their guidance, "turn then thy face in the direction of the sacred Mosque, where ever you are, turn your faces that direction."

Sura 2: 273 and 274 state that Charity is only for those in need of something "tangible" according to the Qur'an. Where in the Bible explains Charity as "Love" See Matthew 19: 19 "Love they neighbors as thyself".

Sura 3: 2 and 3 state with Allah, there is no god but he,, and again in Sura 3: 18, there is no god but he,,, yet the Qur'an states many places "we" created man, and Sura 15: 26, 28, 29 "WE" raise up the dead, also Sura 7: 57.

Sura 3: 45 and 47 state that Mary had glad tidings, that Christ Jesus will be born in honor in this world and the hereafter, (meaning Believers of Jesus Christ)
also Sura 3: 46 Jesus will be of the Company of the "Righteous".
It is very easy to see that the person who was putting the Qur'an together, was reading the Bible. And putting his own twist in the Qur'an.

Sura 3: 49 States, Jesus Christ is appointed a messenger TO the children of Israel and also that Jesus does healing and brings the "Dead into Life". ((No One but a True God can bring the Dead into Life)). Satan cannot deny this...

I once asked a Muslim person why the Qur'an states that Jesus healed and brought the dead to life, and he said,, Allah allowed Jesus to do that,, I then asked him if he thought Allah was tired.

Sura 43: 64, states, Fear Allah, and obey me. At this point one must take the word "fear" seriously, meaning "awareness of danger" For a Muslim.

Sura 3: 50, States, Jesus Christ comes as a sign from the Lord, and that sign is God the Father, it is easy to see that Satan has to follow a system when writing a book.

Sura 3: 51 states, Jesus Christ is called the "Way is Straight" Taken from the bible see Matthew 3: 3 and John 1: 23 also Heb. 12: 13.

Sura 3: 49, clearly states that Jesus Christ does many miracles which should show any one that ONLY a True God does miracles, in the bible see John 2: 11, 23 and 6: 2 Sura 3: 59 and 22: 5, also 23: 13. State that Jesus is the "Likeness" before God, the second Adam, and that Adam , the first Adam, was created from dust.

Sura 22: 6 state that Allah is the "reality" and it is he who gives life to the dead, yet in Sura 3: 49, states again that Jesus was appointed to the children of Israel, and Jesus was made out of clay and the figure of a bird and became a bird, and Jesus will heal the blind and lepers and bring the dead to life,

that idea was some what taken from the bible in Luke 7: 14 and 15. With a twist.

Sure 3: 106 states that faces lite up with white and black, yet it is not possible that black can light up, just like it is not possible that a True God can lie, but those with black rejected faith, having NO LIGHT on them which is Jesus Christ.

Sura 3: 132 states Muslims have "TWO" to obey,, Allah AND his messenger, also Sura 4: 59, 24: 54, 56. 36: 20 and 64: 12 say the same things. ((Two gods to obey.))

Sura 4: 11 states that "Inheritance" is divided not equal, the male Muslims is to receive "Twice" that of a female.

Sura 4: 34 state it is Allah's permission that you "Muslim men" can "Beat" a woman into obedience.

Sura 4: 157 states that a believer should not kill a believer, "Except by mistake", now how convenient is that I ask.

Sura 4: 171 states that Christ Jesus was no more then a messenger of Allah and his word. However the Holy Spirit proceeding from Jesus, but say not "Three" because Allah is above having a son. But we must wonder what "we and us" are doing in the Qur'an when talking about god and his attributes from Allah.

Sura 5: 12 here Allah made a covenant with the children of Israel and "we" appointed "Twelve" disciples. In the Bible looking at the New Testament is clear many places that Jesus Christ appointed "His Chosen Twelve" see Mark 3: 13.

Sura 5: 75 states Christ the Son of Mary was no more than a messenger, yet in Sura 3: 49 Jesus Christ gave life to the dead and have done miracles,
Sura 6: 47 states that Azar is Abraham's father, however the Bible states in Genesis 11: 27 records Terah begot Abraham, maybe the Qur'an is talking about a different Abraham.

Sura 7: 40 states to those who reject "OUR SIGN" and treat with arrogance, no opening will there be of the gates of heaven nor will they enter the "Garden" until the Camel can pass through the eye of the needle, such is "Our Reward" for those in sin. It is clear that you have two places to go, heaven or the garden, along with this, "our Sign" in the Qur'an. It looks like the Qur'an is talking about Allah and his partner god, the messenger. Also the eye of the needle phrase came from the Bible, see Matthew 19: 24.

Sura 9: 5 is clear that Muslims are to slay, "Kill" the ones they call Pagans who do not accept their religion, "Where ever you find them" and seize them "beleaguer them" meaning to harass them with difficulties and lie in wait for them making "War".

Sura 9: 29 here it is clear, "Fight those who believe not in Allah nor the last day" nor hold that forbidden which hath been forbidden by Allah "and" his messenger, nor "acknowledge" the religion of "TRUTH" form among the people of the Book "Bible" until they "Pay" a price with willing submission.
This passage is admitting that the Bible of Jesus Christ is the Book of Truth.

Sura 9: 30 states the Jews call "Uzair a son of Allah" This is made up and false, the Jews have never made this statement, moreover the Jews know that Allah is a false god.

Muslims say that Christians call Jesus Christ the Son of Allah, Christians know with out doubt that Christ Jesus is the "Only Begotten" Son of God the Father through the Holy Spirit, see Matthew 1: 18. Mary's first born child called Jesus of the Holy Spirit.
Sura 3: 45 will admit that Mary gave birth to Christ Jesus, held in honor in the World and the Here After.

Sura 6: 101 states how can God have a Son when he has "No Consort?" To Christians the word consort means, "In agreement or harmonize". It is clear the Holy Spirit is in "Total Harmony" with God the Father through out the Bible, the Word of God and Spirit. It is also clear that Satan is making challenge against the bible in the Qur'an and using the Muslims or any one else who is not a believer in Christ Jesus to follow Satan.

Sura 19: 20 and 3: 47 states Mary said, O My Lord, how shall I have a son when no man hath touched me?, The answer is recorded in the Bible under Matthew 1: 18 "By the Holy Spirit". Any Muslim I talk with, will not believe there is a Holy Spirit, and yet in Sura 2: 87 the Holy Spirit was given to Jesus to strengthen Him, Muslims only believe what they are told by their messengers.

Sura 9: 111 is giving a statement that the Truth is in the "Torah" the Gospel, which is the Christian Bible, and the Qur'an. However the Qur'an can be completely discounted because it is clear that the people of God the Father have NOTHING to do with the Qur'an or any book from the Islam religion. God allowed the Qur'an to give us a choice just as He did with Adam and Eve in their garden.

Sura 15: 28 – 30 states that Adam was fashioned, and after that Angles where to treat Adam like a god, as it says, "fall you down in obeisance unto him" to submit to him and the angles prostrated themselves to Adam as their God, except Lblis, who is the devil. So Allah put a curse on the devil until judgment day, Sura 15: 35 states, and the curse shall be on thee till the day of judgment, How odd this is, because after that, it clearly says that the devil will be forgiven if only until judgment day.

Sura 17: 111 states that Allah begets no son, "no partner" yet Allah talks about "we or us" which is a definite contradiction, also see Sura 16: 102 and 17: 85 where Allah talks about the Holy Spirit to the believers as a messenger and as a guide and glad tidings to Muslims.

Sura 19: 23 states that Mary gave birth under a Palm Tree. This is totally false, History records in the Bible that Jesus was born in a house or stable in Bethlehem, see Matthew 2: 11

In the Bible, Leviticus 11: 7 state that "Swine" are unclean and cannot be eaten, this was for Old Testament Jews under the Law, however, this was changed by Jesus in the New Testament, not being under the Law with Peter in Acts 10: 14 and 15, the Qur'an states in Sura 6: 145 the flesh of swine is a abomination.

Sura 6: 151 states not to kill your children on a plea of want, in fact don't kill any one "Except by Justice: or if it be the Law, that sure give Muslims lots of room to act.

It is Ironic to read Sura 6: 154, that "we gave Moses the book" first of all, who is "we" and second, the book of Moses was the Mosaic Law given by God the Father thousands of years before Islam, or Mahammad.

The Bible in Genesis 2: 16 – 17 states God commanded Adam not to eat from the tree of knowledge of good and evil and Adam, in Gen. 3: 1 explained to Eve what God wanted. You shall not eat of every tree of the garden, but Satan persuaded Eve to eat, and Eve persuaded Adam and in Gen. 3: 7 they found to be naked and sewed fig leaves to cover themselves. Now Satan knows that this is true, but in Sura 7: 22 it states, that by eating of this tree they become naked and did sew leaves for a cover. What is interesting is that Satan could not call the True God "Allah" as in Sura 7: 23, they said, "Our Lord" we have wronged our own souls.

The Bible in Genesis 2: 2 States God said He ended His Work from which He had made the heavens and the earth. Satan cannot deny this, See Sura 7: 54, it states God "not Allah" created the heavens and the earth in "six days".

Sura 7: 55 states Allah loves not those who trespass beyond bounds, "This statement is understood for a false god" Simply the Muslims god "Allah" cannot love a sinner only because Allah is not a "true God" The Bible states in John 3: 16. For God so Loved the World that He gave His ONLY Begotten Son that who so ever believeth in Him should not perish but have everlasting life.

Sura 7: 103 states that Moses rescued the children of Israel from Pharaoh. This goes on with mass confusion about what Moses did in the Qur'an

Sura 7: 126 talks about Muslims who "bow to the will" . Interesting at that time, there were no Muslims in existence. Sura 7: 157 talks about the Taurat, what ever that is, and the New Testament Gospel which did not exist at that time during Moses time, which is Salvation under Grace explained. In the Bible, starting with Exodus 1: 1 through 34, and all through Exodus you will find the True recording of Moses and what had happened to the children of Israel.

The Qur'an has gross "contradictions" for Muslims, for example Sura 17: 33 do not take life which Allah has made sacred, except for just cause, and for any one who is slain wrongfully, we have given his inherited authority to forgive. So it seems here, if your wrong from killing anyone, you have the inherited forgiveness.

Sura 9: 5 states Muslims are to kill the Pagans "nonbelievers" where ever you find them. This is clearly "Jihad" in any land, the Muslim holy war, called the justified killing by Allah.

Sura 9: 29 states "Fight" those who believe not Allah nor the last day, nor hold that forbidden which hath been for bidden by Allah and his messenger, nor acknowledge the religion of "TRUTH". NOW look here, what religion of Truth is the Qur'an talking about?. The Qur'an is obviously making a statement that the Muslims religion is "FALSE" and that there is a religion known as the "TRUTH" Being from Jesus Christ.

Sura 9: 30 states the Jews call "Uzair" the son of Allah, and the Christian call Christ the Son of Allah, and so, Allah's curse is on them, How Ironic is that ?

Sura 9: 38 here is what makes "Jihad" a killer at large. It states, O you who believe, what is the matter with you that when you are asked to go forth in the cause of Allah, you cling heavily to the earth? Do you prefer the life of this world to the hereafter? But little is the comfort of this life as compare with the hereafter.
It is easy to see, the Qur'an (Through Satan) Is brain washing Muslims to give up their life to kill others and destroy anyone who is not a believer of their Cult religion.

Now here come the "Threat from Allah" See Sura 9: 39 unless you go forth, he will punish you with a grievous penalty and put others in your place.
So one must wonder, is it better to live in hell, or on earth.

Sura 9: 44 those who believe in Allah and the last day ask thee for "no exemption from fighting" With their goods and persons and Allah knoweth those who do their duty. Sura 9: 61 states in part, those who molest "annoy" the prophet will have a grievous chastisement. (talk about a threat)
Sura 9: 62 it is more fitting that they; should please Allah "and" his messenger, if they are believers.

Sura 9: 63 states, know they not that for those who oppose Allah "and" his messenger, is the fire of hell?

17

Sura 9: 66 states, make no excuses, you have rejected faith after you had excepted it, if we pardon some of you, we will punish others amongst you for that they are sinners.

Sura 9: 67 The Hypocrites hath forgotten Allah, so he hath forgotten them.

Sura 9: 69 their works are fruitless in this world and in the hereafter and they are the losers.

Sura 9: 74 they swear by Allah that they said nothing "evil" but indeed they uttered blasphemy and they uttered it after accepting Islam, and they meditated a plot which they were unable to carry out. Now this is getting good, it is clear that the Muslim god is an unforgiving god, unless you become a killer, many places in the Qur'an it states that Allah is often forgiving and most merciful in Sura *; 69. 9: 91 and 9: 102.

As you can see Sura 9: 80 states whether you ask for forgiveness or not, "there sin is unforgivable" Which is not known but if you ask seventy times for forgiveness, Allah will not forgive them, because they have rejected Allah and his messenger, and Allah guides not those who were perversely rebellious. This would be a far cry from being Allah in Sura 55: 1 which states, in the name of Allah, most gracious, and most merciful.

Clearly, Jihad " the holy war" Of Islam is at your door step to anyone who will not accept to be a Muslim in this world of religions. Now here is a Hypothesis made by Muslims, Sura 9: 111 states Allah has purchased of the believers their person and their goods. For theirs "in return" is the Garden of Paradise, they "Muslims" fight in his name "Allah" and kill and be killed. A promise binding on him in truth. Through the Torah, the Gospel and the Qur'an. And who is more faithful to his covenant then Allah? Then rejoice in the "Bargain" which you have concluded, that is the achievement supreme. "This definitely is a brain wash!".

Sura 9: 123 continues with hate and war against who will not except Islamic beliefs, O you who believe! "Fight the unbelievers" Who are near to you and let them find harshness in you, and know that Allah is with those who fear him. This clearly shows how deceitful the Qur'an is, Sura 10: 3 states Allah created heavens and earth in six days, and then Sura 41: 9 and 12 states Allah created earth and firmaments in two days, but took the measured sustenance in four days.

ALL these readings in this so called religious Qur'an book, is the writing of Satan himself, I have noticed that some parts are to look good for some, but the "Majority" of this Qur'an is directed into "Killing anyone" who will not worship Allah.
Let me show you how Satan can be so very brilliantly stupid to an "Almighty God" the only True God Christians follow.

Reading Sura 10: 3 it states Truly your lord is Allah,, who created the heavens and earth in six days, Then he established himself on the throne, regulating and governing all things. But for Christians, God the Father is and ever will b eon the Throne, He had "Never" left the Throne or will ever leave the Throne, governing all things at all times, above all. Here is some thing interesting, when I read Sura 10: 31 it states, who is it that brings out the living from the dead and the dead from the living?, and who is it that rules and regulates all affairs ? " They will soon say Allah".

True Christians know from the beginning of man, that God the Father rules over All, and is ALL, and Satan will fight this until Jesus returns to put him away.
Sura 22: 6 23: 80 and 30: 19 all state, "this is so, because Allah is the reality, for Muslims anyway, it is he who gives life to the dead and it is he who has power over all things.
Sura 3: 48, 49 states, Allah will teach "Jesus" the book and wisdom, the Torah and Gospel, and will appoint Him a messenger to Israel, " the Qur'an was left out here".

Ironically for Muslims, the Gospel is Jesus Christ Himself, and Jesus is the ONLY Instrument of the Bible, for He is the Word of Truth, which the Qur'an states, and Satan cannot deny.

Sura 30: 49 states, and appointed him "Jesus" a messenger to the children of Israel with this message, I have come to you with a sign from your Lord, in that I make for you out of clay as it were, the figure of a bird and breathe into it and it becomes a bird, "by Allah's leave" And I heal those born blind and lepers and I bring the dead into life, "By Allah's leave". It must be so,,, Allah is on vacation....

It looks here being Allah on leave, has given Jesus power to perform miracles for a reason unknown, but easy to see, Satan cannot deny the One True God, Jesus Christ as God. However, it is odd, Allah does not give the same rights to his other messengers.

First of all, all the birds that were made from the beginning by God the Father. Second, it seems Allah was in a big need for a vacation, so he went on leave, putting Jesus in charge so to speak, can you imagine God taking a vacation? And only one with all power and understanding " In need of vacation" Muslims need to know how "Duped" they really are and have been for thousands of years.

Sura 10: 90 states interesting parts, "I believe that there is no god except Him whom the Children of Israel believe in" I am of those who submit "to Allah in Islam" In the Bible the record is clear, that the children of Israel, "the Jews" believe in Jehovah, the ONE and only True God, and also to this day, See Exodus 6: 3

Sura 11: 43 states that Noah talked about Allah and his command, yet there is no evidence that Allah was ever recorded then, by Islam, Although Muslims like to "think" that Allah was a god of heaven and earth, but they have nothing to back up their beliefs,

Further it states that one of Noah's son's drowned and was not on the Ark yet the Bible records in Gen 6: 18. Is truth thousands of years before Islam become a known religion.

Sira 11: 48 states, the words came, O Noah ! Come down from the Ark with peace form "us" Obviously Satan cannot refute that the Trinity exists and this is why you will see "us and we" in the Qur'an, many times over and over, but of course Allah does not talk about his messengers, must that they are messengers of some sort, and that could be any body, But then,,, any Muslims can stand up and claim to be a messenger. And claim the same power is Allah, the false god of no power but cheap talk.

Sura 15: 23 states, and verily, it is "we" who gave life, and who give death, it is "we" who remain inheritors, after all else passes away. This is really odd, here is says Allah will give back after all is done, but the God of Israel is ownership of all things from beginning to end.

Sura 15: 29 states, when I have fashioned "him" in due proportion and breathed into him my spirit, here Allah is talking about the First Adam, taken from the Bible of course, Gen. 2: 7
Sura 15: 74 states , and "we" turned "the Cities" upside down and rained down on them brimstone hard as baked clay. Taken from Gen. 13: 10 "Sodom and Gomorrah" destruction.

Sura 15: 81 States, "we" sent them "our signs" But they persisted in turning away from them. Sura 15: 85 "we" created NOT the heavens, the earth and all between them,, but for just ends. This is very odd, Sura 10: 3 states, the heavens and earth was created by Allah. Looks like Satan can't make up his mind.

Sura 15: 97 states, "we" do indeed know how the heart is distressed at what they say, a simple question, If Allah is but "one god" then why does Allah need "we and us".

Sura 16: 4 states, he has created man from a " sperm-drop and behold this same man becomes an open disputer". How interesting that Allah used a sperm to create the first or second Adam, in Sura 3: 47 states that, she "Mary" said, O my Lord, how shall I have a son when no man hath touched me? And Allah said, "even so" Allah creates what he willeth, when he hath decreed a matter, he but saith to it "be" and it is.

Could it be, Allah forgot the sperm-drop concept, or that the first Adam was made of earth, and the second Adam was from the Holy Spirit ?.

The introduction to Sura 12 states, that Joseph, the son of Jacob, the Qur'an's story is similar but not identical with the bible. This is totally false in the Qur'an, who ever has written the Qur'an was reading the bible and making up his own twisted stories for the Qur'an from time to time.

Sura 14: 8 States in part, and Moses said, "if you show ingratitude" you and all on earth together – yet is Allah free of al wants, well then, why is it in Sura 30: 49. Allah needed a "vacation" And put himself on leave giving Jesus the power?.

It is well known that Muslims believe that "Allah" is but one god, and only one god, we Sura 16: 51 states, Allah has said, "Take not for worship two gods for he is just one god, then fear me " and me alone".

Looking at Sura 15: 8 in part, "We" send not the angles down except for just cause, Sura 15: 9 "we" have with out doubt sent down the messenger, and we absurdly guard it from corruption. Sura 15: 12 even so do "we" let it creep into the hearts of the sinners.

Sura 15: 14 even so "we" opened out to them a gate from heaven, and were to continue "all day" ascending there in.

Sura 15: 16 it is "we" who have set out constellations in the heavens and made them fair seeming to "all" beholders.

Sura 15: 17 and moreover "we" Have guarded them from every accursed Satan.

I am wondering here, who the guarded are, could be the brain washed ones.

Sura 15: 19 and the earth, "we" have spread out like a carpet.

Sura 15: 20 And "we" have provided therein means of subsistence

Sura 15: 21 And there is not a thing but its sources and treasures inexhaustible are with "us" but "we" only send down thereof in due and ascertainable measures.

Sura 15: 22 and "we" Send the fecundating winds, then cause the rain to decent from the sky.

Sura 17: 44 and 78: 12 states in part, "the Seven Heavens" I am wondering how the writer or writers have dreamed this one up. The Bible is clear that there are but three Heavens, see 2 Corinthians 12: 2 Paul went to the abode of God, in the third heaven.

Sura 17: 61. 18: 50 and 20: 116 state in part, behold, "we" said to the angles "prostrate unto Adam: they did prostrated except Lblis. However, it does not state if this was the first Adam or the Second Adam, (' I'm sure there confused)

Now here is a weird Qur'an contradiction, as you know to "prostrate is to worship" but several Sura's state Allah is the only one god. See Sura 2: 133 One "true god" to him do we submit.

Sura 2: 163 And your god is one god, there is no god but he, most gracious, most merciful.

Sura 23: 23 in part, Oh my people ! "Worship Allah" you have no other god but him. Why is it, the Angles were commanded to prostrate " worship" to Adam? When other Sura's say to worship Allah only.

Sura 17: 111 States, say praise to be Allah, who begets no son, and has "no partner" in his dominion, nor "needs" any to protect him from humiliation. Yes, magnify him for his greatness and glory, (what ? No partner, lets check this out.)
Sura 9: 90 and 94 State, Allah, "AND" his messenger.
Sura 3: 32 Obey Allah, "AND" his messenger.
Sura 3: 132 Obey Allah "AND" his messenger.
Sura 4: 171 Jesus, a Messenger of Allah.
Sura 9: 24 Allah "OR" his messenger

Sura 18: 94 States in part. "Gog and Magog" people do great mischief on earth. Notice this information comes from the bible, see Revelation 20: 8 in part, and shall go out to deceive the nations which are in the four quarters of the earth, Gog and Magog, to gather, when together to battle.

Sura 19: 17 and 19 state, "we" sent to her our Angel, he said nay, I am only a messenger form the Lord to announce to thee the gift of a "PURE SON" here Satan cannot deny that Jesus Christ was the ONLY Human born of God the Father, Free and Pure from Sin.

Sura 19: 29 state, But she, Mary pointed to the babe, they said "how can we talk to one who is a child in the cradle ?.
Sura 19: 30, 31, 32, 33, and 34. States, he said, I am indeed a servant of Allah, he has given me relegation and made me a prophet, and he has enjoyed on me prayer and zakat as long as I live. He has made me kind to my mother and not over bearing or unblest, so peace is on me the day I was born, the day that I die, and they day I shall be raised up to life again, such was Jesus the son of Mary, it is a statement of truth which they vainly dispute.

This statement made, is so ridiculous, it could be understood as insane, and deceptive, Satan is trying is best to make it look like the Christian Savior, who came as a new born babe, born of a Virgin. Satan would like that Jesus is talking about Allah undisputed.

The Bible records that Abram's second wife, "Hagar" conceived. And Hagar was despised by Sarai, Abram's first wife who could not bear children for Abram. See Gen. 16: 3, 4, and 5. In the Bible, Genesis 16: 11 and 12 here the Lord delivered a message to Hagar, telling her that she is going to have a son, and that his name will be "Ishmael" And that he will be a "Wild man" and his hand will be against ever man, and every man will be against him, and he will dwell in the presence of his kind. "Which is the case today, and will be forever."

God changed Abram's name to "Abraham" after Ishmael was born, and God told Abraham that Sarai and Abraham would have a son, and his name would be "Isaac" and Sarai's name was changed to Sarah, God said, she will bear a son, and God will establish "His Covenant with Isaac" for an everlasting covenant, and with Isaac's seed after him, see Genesis 17: 5 – 19.

But as far as Ishmael, God had blessed him to be fruitful and will multiply exceedingly, Twelve princes shall be beget. " This is to say Twelve great nations" but the covenant will be established with ONLY Isaac and his generations, but not Ishmael, see Gen. 17: 20 and 21.

Most places in the Qur'an it is difficult to follow, Sura 21: 71 talks about Abraham and Lot was sent to a land blessed for nations. And Sura 21: 72 states Isaac and Jacob came into this picture and then Sura 21: 76 states Noah and his family was delivered from a great distress, (an earthly flood) These time periods are hundreds if not thousands of years apart. In most places in the Qur'an, Allah who is a god of Muslims, will keep explaining that he is connected to some one other then himself. But look at this,

Sura 21: 66 states, Abraham said, "Do you then worship, besides Allah, things that can neither be of any good to you nor do you harm? Then reading, Sura 21:73 states "We" made them leaders, building men "by OUR command" and "we" inspired them to do good deeds, to establish regular prayers, and to give zakat and they constantly served "us" and Us only.

Sura 21: 79 states, to Solomon "we" inspired the " right understanding of the matter" it was "we" who did all these things.
Sura 21: 82 states, it was "we" who guarded them. (talking about Solomon and David)
Sura 21: 84 states, "we" removed the distress that was on him. (David)
Sura 21: 88, states, so "we" listened to him and delivered him from distress and thus do "we" deliver those who have faith.
Sura 21: 90 states, so "we listened to him and "we" granted him Yahya.(what ever that is) and "We" cured his wife barrenness from him. They used to call on "us" in yearing and awe and humble themselves before "us".

Now this one is really good, reading Sura 21: 91 states, and remember her who guarded her chastity; "we" breathed into her from ((Our Spirit)) and "we" made her and her son a sign for all peoples. Here the Qur'an apparently is talking about Jesus, but it does not say outright.

Sura 21: 104 states, the day that "we" roll up the heavens like a scroll rolled up for books Completed even as "we" produced the first creation, so shall "we" produce a new one, A promise "we" have undertaken. Truly shall "we" have undertaken, truly shall "we" fulfil it.
Sura 21: 105 states, before this "we" wrote in the Psalms, (NOW This is Odd, Allah and his gods actually say that they wrote some of the Bible.)

In the Qur'an, Satan cannot, and will not deny that God has a Holy Trinity, even with all the deceitful teachings he records, he must follow the Truth of the name of God, by command, God the Father – God the Son - God the Holy Spirit, three in ONE.

And this being true as it is written, is why you will see all the "we" and "us" appear, however, will deny that Allah is connected in any way to anyone, The Qur'an is extremely hard to follow for anyone, this is why they are instructed to hear and obey the "messengers" at any and all times, and at any place, and if they turn from this religion, they must face DEATH at some time in their life by other Muslims them selves.

The Qur'an has proven gross contradictions and fraudulent representations, namely of a false god who is called Allah, and his deceitful teachings through the messenger.

Remember, a Muslim is ordered by Allah, through his messenger's to give up his life in order to obey Allah. By the way of killing the unbelievers where ever he finds them. Any one can see that this is a "Religion of Death" and your death to be more accurate.

Christianity is worldly known as the "Religion of ever lasting Love" And hated by Satan.

Sura 22: 5 and 23: 13, 14 states, "we" created you out of dust, then out of Sperm, then out of a leech – like – clot, then out of a morsel of flesh, partly formed and partly unformed, in order that "we" may manifest " Our Power" to you," And "we" cause whom "we" will to rest in the wombs for an appointed term. Then so "we" bring you out of babes, then "foster you" that you may reach your age of full strength.

Sura 22: 5 is in direct contradiction to Sura 2: 117, which states, the originator of the heavens and the earth, when he decreed a matter, he saith to it "BE" and it is. Where as, why would a god go through all this dust, sperm, leech, clot and flesh, when all he has to say is "Be", and it is ..

But then, Sura 3: 49 states Allah takes a "vacation" or on leave, and Jesus pops into the picture for him,, being appointed a messenger to the children of Israel, "NOT ALLAH" giving life, healing the blind and bringing the dead to life. Again, Satan cannot deny this Ironically, Allah cannot do his work " alone, But then, you have to give wonder, if you read Sura 22: 31 which states, Being true in faith to Allah, and NEVER assigning partners to him, if any one assigns partners to Allah, he is as if he had fallen from heaven and been snatched up by birds, or the wind had swooped like a bird on its prey, and thrown him into a far distant place, Now reading Sura 15: 10 states, "we" did send messengers before thee amongst the sects of old., Sura 15: 23 states, and verily, it is "we" who give life, and who give death, it is "we" who remain inheritors, after all else passes away. (sure sounds like partners here) Sura 9: 24, state, Allah, "OR" his messenger.
Sura 24: 47, 50, 52, 54, and 62 all state in part, we believe in Allah, "AND" in the Messenger, and more so, Allah "AND" his messenger will deal unjustly with them. Yes, it actually states, Allah will deal "UNJUSTLY" I don't think you would want a false god to deal JUSTLY now, would you ?

Sura 60: 4 states in part, Unless you believe in Allah and "HIM ALONE"
Obviously "Him Alone" must be fraudulent meaning, or is it "We and Us" .
Sura 25: 2 states in part, he to whom belongs the dominion of the heavens and earth, no son has he begotten, nor has he a partner in his dominion.
well now, if Allah has NO Partner, then who is the messenger?

Sura 33: 57 states, those who "Annoy Allah AND his messenger" Allah has cursed them in this world and in the hereafter. And has prepared for them a humiliating punishment.

Sura 33: 60, 61, 62, and 64 all state, the unbelievers shall have a curse on them, wherever they are found, "They shall be seized and killed" such was the practice "Approved of Allah" among those who lived afore time. "No Change" wilt thou find in the practice approved of Allah, verily, Allah has cursed the unbelievers and prepared for them a blazing fire.

If Jews, or Christians believe that they are safe where ever you live, you best think again, because Muslims are all over the world who can carry out Allah's wishes in time to come.

Sura 29: 6 states in part, Allah is free of "ALL NEEDS form ALL Creation"
Sura 31: 12 states in part, Allah is free of "ALL Wants".
Sura 60: 6 states in part, for those whose hope is in Allah and The last day, but if any turn away truly Allah is free of all wants, worthy of all praise.
If the Qur'an had "any truth" to it, then why is it Allah wants the "Unbelievers cursed" seized and killed, Seems this fake god wants any person who rejects him, should be killed.

Satan is always working with them who lives for EVIL, and wants any person who reject him to be killed, and not die a natural death of any sort. This also is a motive to dominate the world for the sake of Islam, the EVIL religion of Muslims.

Sura 37: 2 states those "Muslims" who are strong in repelling "evil" it is clear that the Islam religion does not believe killing another is "EVIL" and if you are a nonbeliever, then you are considered evil to a Muslim.

Sura 38: 5 states, has he made gods "ALL" into ONE GOD? This truly is a strange statement, This is strange only to the ones who follow Satan "Or Allah," Think about "Water" as being three things in ONE, "Steam – Ice – and Liquid" All these are ONE, so why is it not possible in the TRUE GOD, to proclaim and bring forth three Divine Persons in " ONE GOD". This is not believed in the Muslim world, however, in the Qur'an it gives you the fact that God cannot be denied in the Divinity because it's in print hundreds of times, as "WE and US" being more then ONE. But Not connected to God the Father in any way, shape or form.

Muslims have never understood from the beginning of their time, that the Word of God, the Bible, clearly gives record in Genesis 1: 26 God said, let "US" make man in "Our Image" "US" meaning more then "ONE" And this DOES NOT Mean any so called messenger over and over, or any one just proclaiming to be a messenger as in the Muslim world.

Sura 38: 45, 46 and 47 all state, And commemorate our servants, Abraham, Isaac and Jacob, possessors of power and vision. (No MENTION OF ISHMAEL,) There founder.
And the reason " Ishmael" was left out, is because he was not put under the Covenant Promise of God the Father, see Genesis 17: 21

Sura 38: 36 states, verily "WE" did choose them for a special "Purpose" the remembrance of the hear after.
Sura 38: 47 state, they were in "OUR" sight, truly of the company of the "ELECT" and the good.
This is the Only Time, "ELECT" is used in the Qur'an, in were it signifies God the Father chosen people in the New Testament Bible seventeen times.

Sura 41: 5 states, , They say, Our harts are under veils, concealed from that to which thou does invite us, and in our ears is a deafness between us and thee is a screen, so do thou what thou wilt, for us we shall do what we will.

Interesting I have talked to Muslims, and they mostly say, "You have your religion, and I have mine". And I say, that's true, but one of us are dead wrong.

Sura 41: 6 clearly states, I am but a man like you, it is revealed to me "Muslim" by inspiration, that your God is One God, so take the straight path unto Him and ask for His forgiveness, and woe to those who join gods of Allah.

I would personally like every Muslim to meet and read this Sura passage and give me their interpretation of this statement separately. That would be interesting indeed.

Sura 41: 39 states in part, Truly He who gives life to the "Dead" earth can surely give life to "men" who are dead, for He has power over ALL things.

This statement "coincides' with Sura 3: 49 As Jesus gives life to the Dead, and has done many miracles.

Sura 45: 16 states, "We" (meaning the Triune God) did afore (meaning the beginning of the Jewish Nations) grant to the Children of Israel (Genesis 17: 20) the Book, (the Bible, the Word of God) The power of command and prophet hood (Covenant of God) "We" gave them for sustenance, things good and pure, and "we" (the Triune God) favored them above the Nations, (and everlasting Covenant.)

Notice in the text, the Islam religion or Muslims are not included here.

Many places it is written in the Qur'an a "Straight Path" is used, which has been extracted from the Bible, see Matthew 3: 3 Mark 1: 3 And Luke 3: 4,

the Qur'an shows in Sura 19: 44 I will guide thee to a way that is even and "Straight". Sura 43: 43 states,, Verily, thou are on a "Straight Way"
Sura 46: 30 states, it guides to the truth and to a "Straight Path".
Sura 22: 74 States, They " the unbelievers" do not have the right estimate of Allah, for Allah is powerful and mighty.
Sura 22: 75 state, Allah chooses messengers from Angels and from men for Allah is he who hears and sees all things.

If a Muslim god has all this power and might, why is it he needs to "Choose" messengers from Angels, " is one angel better then another ?.
And why does Allah need men to hear and see for him, I thought it was said he has all this power and might? In Sura 22: 74. Also Sura 49: 1 states, Allah is he who hears and knows all things. And check this one,,, Sura 47: 38 Allah is FREE of "ALL WANTS".

Sura 48: 29 states, Muhammad is the messenger of Allah, it would be very easy for anyone to proclaim themselves to being a messenger today, as well as in the time of Muhammad, this is the way Cults start. Some people just have some kind of dream or idea that would give them some great attention, it happens all the time and will happen in the future.

The Very reason why we have the bible for our guidance, is God did not have to re-write the Bible, nor did he make mistakes, He started with Genesis, and ended it with Revelations. But man in Cult religions do this all the time.
In the Word of God, man seems to put his two cents in it, and this is what gives us confusion, with out the Holy Spirit to guide us, we could not accept or understand His Word. Sura 49: 11 states in part, O you who believe, let not some men among you laugh at others, nor let some women laugh at others, nor call each other nicknames.

Sura 49: 12 in part states, Avoid suspicion as much as possible, for suspicion in some cases is a sin.

Sura 50: 2, 3 states in part, the unbelievers say, "this is a wonderful thing" what, when we die and become dust, "Shall we live again"? That is a Sort of return far from "OUR" understanding.

As you can see, this is understood as not believing in a life after earthly death, It looks like the Muslims are saying "What", However, the Qur'an says in many places that they think they will dwell in heavenly Gardens with rivers flowing, if they kill unbelievers.

Sura 32: 19 states, but those who believe and do righteous deeds are Gardens as hospital homes.

Remember, the deeds of righteousness is the killing of pagans for Allah, see Sura 9: 5 states, Slay the Pagans wherever you find them.

Sura 60: 4 states in part, Abraham and those with him, when they said to their people, "we" are clear of you and of whatever you worship besides Allah, we have rejected you, and there has arisen, between us and you enmity and hatred for ever., unless you believe in Allah and Him alone.

Sura 24: 47 in part, We believe in Allah, "AND" in the messenger.

Sura 24: 50 in part, Allah "AND" his messenger will deal "UNJUSTLY" with them. this looks like Allah has a definite partner to help him out with unjust actons.

Sura 24: 52 In part, Say "Obey Allah "AND" Obey the messenger.

Thousands of years before Muhammad has started his religion, God the Father started in His Word, the Bible, See Galatians 4: 28 and 29, states, Now we brethren, as Isaac was, are the children of Promise, but then he that was born after the flesh, "Islam" persecuted him that was born after the Spirit, "Christians" even so it is now.

The Subject of Divorce is in the Qur'an, in part see Sura 65: 1 when you divorce women, divorce them at their prescribed periods, and count "accurately" their prescribed periods.
No one can explain what a women's period has to do with a divorce, but it gets better.

Sura 65: 2 States, Thus when they fulfil their term appointed, either take them back on equitable terms or part with them on equitable terms.

Sura 65: 4 states, Women who passed the age of monthly courses, if you have any doubt, is three months and for others, it is the same, and if for those who are pregnant, their period is until they deliver.

Every Mulsim has his own interpretation on this subject, as of most of the Qur'an, , which is obviously given through their messenger by their teaching and what ever else they say and do.

Sura 59: 21, 22, 23, and 24 state in part, Allah has sent down this Qur'an on a mountain.
I believe the Muslims think that the Qur'an was sent to Muhammad, but it is known that Muhammad could not "read or write" So that is a problem, but Muslims believe others worked with Muhammad to figure this out. My question is, why would a god who knows ALL THINGS. Send a message to a messenger that can't read or write ?.

Further, Sura 76: 23 states that the Qur'an was sent down in three stages, but we have to guess who the "Three stages are". Because no record is given as to what stage was first or last.

Sura 59: 22, states, Allah is he whom there is no other god, who knows "ALL THINGS" both secret and open, he being most gracious, most merciful.

Sura 59: 23 states, Allah is he, that whom there is no other god, the sovereign, the holy one, the source of peace and perfection, the guardian of faith, the preserver of safety, the exalted in might, the irresistible, the justly proud glory to Allah, High is he, above the partners they attribute to him.

From this message, Allah picks his partners, but I though Allah did not need partners being that he knows all things and needs nothing to get things done, being perfect, Sura 22: 75, 75 states, Allah chooses messengers from angels and men and makes decisions with them.

Sura 59: 24 states, He is Allah, the creator, the originator, the fashioner. To him belong the most beautiful name, whatever is in the heavens and on earth, doth declare his praises and glory, and he is the exalted in might, the wise.

NO PLACE in the Qur'an does it state, that Allah is a God of Genuine LOVE to humanity, in order to be a GOD of LOVE, this GOD must be a TRUE GOD, as the God of Abraham, Isaac and Jacob, "Who is the God of Christianity".

The Bible in John 3: 16 records, for God so LOVED the WORLD, who so ever believeth in His Son will have Everlasting Life.

Sura 4: 157 states in part, "We Killed Christ Jesus the son of Mary" The messenger of Allah. "But they killed him not" nor crucified him. ONLY a Likeness of that was shown to them. And those who differ therein are full of doubt with no certain knowledge. But only conjecture to follow. For of a surety they killed him not.

Sura 4: 158 states, Allah raised Him, "Jesus" up unto HIMSELF.

As you can see, Muslims believe that Jesus Christ "Never Died" but was taken up with Allah, or, that He did Die, but He did come back by Himself. And only a TRUE GOD can do that.

Sura 19: 33 states, Jesus Christ said, peace is on me the day I was born, the day that I die, and the day that I shall be raised up to life again.

The Christian Bible is sent from God the Father, through Jesus Christ, Totally Trustworthy and with out mistake, the ONLY Guide to all humanity in written form, totally True with Facts. Ephesians 2: 8 KJV bible, States, "For by Grace are you saved, through Faith, and that Not of yourself, it is a Gift of God, Not of Works, least any man would boast.

As you can see, Salvation of ALL Humanity is a "Free GIFT" From the One True God.

Now the Qur'an, being an Islamic Religion, is Totally Opposite, see Sura 39: 61, states, But Allah will deliver the righteous for they have "Earned Salvation"
Sure 29: 7 Sura 31: 12 and Sura 57: 24 state in part, Allah is free of all needs from All.
Now if Allah is free of all wants or needs, then tell me why he puts messengers next to him to work a work, additionally Allah needs a Loan, See Sura 75: 18 state, for those who give in charity, men and women, and "LOAN" to ALLAH a beautiful LOAN.

Also see Sura 57: 11 state, who is he that will LOAN to ALLAH a beautiful Loan ? Sura 64: 17 state, IF you "Loan to Allah" a beautiful Loan, he will double it to your "Credit" and he will "Grant you Forgiveness"

36

Here Muslims can actually Pay Money to be forgiven from sin. For Allah "and his messenger" is all thankful most forbearing. (but payback is credit ONLY)

Now here is the opposite of what messengers teach. See Sura 4: 48 States, Allah forgiveth not that partners should be "set up" with him, but he for giveth anything else to whom he please. (get that, anything ELSE) to set up partners with Allah is to devise a sin most heinous indeed.

Sura 42: 51 states in part, Allah speaks to man by sending his message to messengers to be revealed. (now how convenient for messengers).

As for Christians, the message from God the Father and Jesus Christ, is sent by the Holy Spirit, and through His Holy Word, the Bible.

Sura 9: 63 state, know they not that for those who "Oppose Allah "and" his messenger" is the fire of hell?. Wherein they shall dwell. That is the supreme disgrace.
Sura 64: 12

Sura 9: 24 states in part, Say, any of your family or kindreds wealth, commerce or dwellings that have declined, are dearer to you than Allah, "OR" his messenger, or the striving in his cause, then wait until Allah brings about his decision, Allah guides not the rebellious, you will be known as an unbeliever.

Here it is easy to see, if your a looser in your property, and it becomes more important then Allah OR his messenger, then your looked at as a unbeliever, and can be killed.

Sura 9: 94 states, it is your actions that Allah "and" his messenger will observe.

Sura 27: 1 and Sura 28: 2 state, these are verses of the Book "Qur'an" that makes things clear.
Now you have to keep in mind, that every thing in the Qur'an is explained by Allah, BUT only through "his messenger" And it is a grievous sin to reject his messenger, and punished by "Death" to any one who rejects his messenger.

Sura 33: 36 state, it is not fitting for a believer, "man or women" when a matter has been decided by Allah "and" his messenger, to have "Any Option" about their decision. If anyone disobeys Allah "and" his messenger, he is indeed on a clearly wrong path, and can be killed.

Sura 41: 9 states in part, that earth and all the worlds were created in 2 Days.
Gosh, I wonder what the Muslims will do when they read Sura 10: 3 after they read That, cause in Sura 10: 3 states the heavens and earth took six days to create.

Sura 41: 12 states in part, So he completed then as Seven firmaments in two days.
Sura 41: 10 states, Allah measured therein it's sustenance in four days.
Sura 7: 54. 10: 3 and 32: 4 all state in part, your guardian Lord is Allah, who created the heavens and the earth in six days, " seems Sura 41: 9 is a mess"

The Bible records all of the creation of the heavens and earth in Genesis 1: and in Genesis 2: 1 and 2. God records His finish of creation. Thus the heavens and the earth were finished, and all the host of them. And on the Seventh day God ended His work which he had made. Of course Allah, and the Muslims, has serious opposition to His Creation, see Sura 1: 117 states in part, when he decreeth a matter, he saith to it "BE" and it is. "But he didn't say Be what.

Sura 40: 68 states, it is he who gives life and death and when he decided upon an affair he says to it "be" and it is.

Sura 4: 34 states in part, to those women on whose part you fear disloyalty and ill conduct, admonish "reprimand" them first, next, refuse to share their beds, then, Beat them.
It would be "unthinkable" that the Christian's "God the Father" or any of His children would be allowed to "beat" their loved ones into submission. But for Muslims this would be a normal life style to beat their women if they felt they needed to, and given permission by their god Allah, "or" his messenger.

Sura 4: 40 states, Allah is never unjust in the least degree, if there is any good done, Allah will doubleth it, and this will give you a great reward. So if you think that beating your women into submission is good, this would be a reward to yourself by Allah

Sura 22: 15 states, if any think that Allah will not help "Or his messenger" in this world and the hereafter, let him stretch out a rope to the ceiling and cut himself off, "Hang yourself" Then let him see whether his plan will remove that which enrages him, (Allah)
SO, if you believe Allah is of no help, "Simply Kill yourself: Easy fix.

The Qur'an is very clear that Muslim people proclaim and believe in "JIHAD" the Muslim holy war against any unbeliever, and / or, any other religion but Islam.

The Bible is very clear and True in every way, when it recorded that Islam, in Genesis 16: 12. And I quote, (and he will be a wild man, his hand will be against every man, and every man's hand against him, and he shall dwell in the presence of all his brethren.) All through the Qur'an, Muslims stress that if "anyone" will not accept Allah as their god, they must slay the pagans where ever you find them, see Sura 9: 5 in part, states, Fight and Slay the Pagans wherever you find them.

Sura 60: 4 states, we are clear of you and of whatever you worship besides Allah, between us and you enmity and hatred "forever" Unless you believe in Allah and him alone. (wonder what happened to the messenger here, maybe he forgot)

There is "NO OTHER RELIGION" on earth that has a dominate hatred for people who wish to worship there own religion, other then Islam. It is easy to see that Islam is a movement through Satan, And Satan will do anything to strike at the ONE TRUE GOD, Jesus Christ and His People, but Jesus will be triumphal over the second death which will have NO POWER over His Children, see Revelation 20: 6. States , Blessed and Holy is He that hath part in the first resurrection, on such the second death hath no power, but they shall be priest of God and Christ.

In the Bible, see 2 Thessalonians 2: 7 and 8. States, for the mystery of iniquity doth already work. Only He who now letteth will let, until he be taken out of the way. And then shall that wicked be revealed, whom the Lord shall consume with the Spirit of His Mouth, and shall destroy with the brightness of His coming.

Sura 15: 28, 39, and 30 also Sura 38: 71 and 72. states that Allah told the angels he was crating man " Adam" from clay, and breathed into him his spirit. At that point, the angels were to fall down in "worship" unto him "Adam".
This looks to be the First Adam, which is a great sin to act out.
However, Sura 16: 51 states " Worship me alone" which is a direct contradiction in the Qur'an

Sura 40: 84 states, we believe in Allah, the one god, and we reject the partners we used to join with him, well now,,, what happened to the "we and us" and what did he do with the messengers?.

Muslims would like to "think" that Christians believe in Allah, but they are farthest from the Truth, moreover, they would like to think that "us Christians" have rejected that Trinity, Which is still farthest from the Truth.
IF they would read the Qur'an and questioned the verses, they would learn form Christians that they have been deceived from their messengers and their false god Allah.

Sura 23: 91, Sura 16: 102 and Sura 23: 44 all state, Allah and his team "WE" sent messengers to be "Obeyed", and if not followed they would be punished.
Sura 15: 10 states that "we" did send messengers before thee and are not to be disobeyed, "OR" Sura 72: 23, states, Be sent to hell. (of course, that's where Allah is as Satan)

It is strange the 10 Commandments are not mentioned in the Qur'an. As Moses is talked about in Sura 7: 154, alone with the Tablets, Of course, Allah allows Muslims to do what the Tablets , or Commandments forbids, and Satan would not like anything made by the One and only True God to show up in the Qur'an.

Sura 21: 108 and Sura 23: 31 state, "God is ONE GOD" and denies my partners, but the Qur'an is FULL of Allah talking about "WE" or US" on and on.
See Sura 40: 84. Which states, We believe in Allah but reject the Partners (messengers)

Sura 61: 6 states, that Jesus, the Son of Mary, speaks only to the Children of Israel, and that a messenger would be sent after Him... which is the Holy Spirit according to the bible.
It is very clear, Satan cannot deny the ONE and ONLY TRUE GOD of all humanity.

See John 14: 26 states, but the Comforter, which is the Holy Spirit whom the Father will send in My Name, He shall teach you all things. And bring all things to your remembrance whatsoever I have said unto you.

Sura 49: 11 states, Muslims are not allowed to "Laugh" or call "nick names"
I would think this would make for a Dull life.

Sura 49: 12 states, Muslims must avoid "suspicion" which makes them totally venerable to believing anything they are told by their messengers.
However, I would think they have lots of suspicion on other religions they know nothing about.

Poetry is a blessing from Our Lord. Poetry is telling some one a story in a rhyming verse. However, Muslims are "forbidden" to take any part in poetry. According to Sura 36: 69. Sura 63: 1 to 6 talks about messengers that are not messengers, and the ONLY Way you can tell if they are true or not, is when they pray "for our forgiveness and turn aside their heads, this makes them not true messengers, and if a Muslim asks Allah to forgive them, Allah " will not forgive them". Yet most ever Sura says Allah is MOST MERCIFUL.

Sura 19: 23 states, that Mary, the Mother of Jesus, delivered her first born Son under a Palm Tree. This is totally false,, in the Bible. Luke 2: 7 records that she wrapped Him in swaddling clothes and laid Him in a "manger". A manger is a trough or open box for livestock feed. Because there was no room for them at the inn. It is clear they were in a "stable" at the time of birth. And not in the open. Sura 19: 29 states that Jesus was in a "cradle".

Muslim me treat their women with malicious and contemptible treatment, only because their god Allah has given them permission as the Qur'an States. See Sura 27: 13 which states, Muslim women are not allowed to pray with men, and any time Muslims pray, they are to "Face the direction of the great Mosque". Real easy to see what they worship. See Sura 2: 144, 149, 150, and 177.

Muslim men have been seen wearing long dresses and a turban most times. Arabs wear what looks like a table cloth over their heads so to speak. This comes from Sura 24: 30 where it states, believing men should lower their gaze "Glare of eyes" and guard their modesty which makes for them a "greater purity" Which Allah acquainted them with all to do.

Muslim men are the " Rules" over Muslim women, All Muslim women wear veils and long dresses, by the command of a man, and some times seen wearing the "Burka" which coves them "Completely" and if a man considers a women "Lewd" Which is with out covering, and if the men feel it is not according to their likings, then women are "or can be" condemned to "death" but usually beaten first. According to Sura 4: 15.

Sura 2: 65 and Sura 7: 166 states, if a Muslim transgresses the Sabbath, they are considered to be " Apes."
Muslim men are allowed to marry up to "Four Times" or having Four wives at one time, unlike that of a Muslim women who is not allowed to pick her own husband. But only men marry women, this is clearly "Adultery" having more then one wife.

In the Bible, Jesus explained His commandments clearly, Matthew 19: 18 states in part, "Thou shalt Not Commit Adultery" This can be understood form the beginning when Adam was given Eve for a wife, if God intended man to have more then one wife, He would have given Adam more than then one wife at that time.

Sura 29: 8 and Sura 31: 15 state, If Muslims lack knowledge in something, and their Parents want to teach them, the Qur'an states, "Obey them Not".

Sura 33: 53 and 57 states, to annoy Allah and his messenger is to be cursed by Allah. Sura 4: 43 and Sura 5: 6 state, when ever a Muslim goes to prayer, they are to first wash themselves by command. When I was at my place of employment, working with Muslims, they would take time out for prayer, they would go to the rest room to wash, although the company installed a shower room for this Muslim activity, they never used the shower. Instead with their clothes on, they would "Splash water" all over themselves making a Real Big Mess for anyone near by.

Sura 20: 12 stats that Muslims are to remove their shoes before prayer, "supposably" they are in a sacred valley called, "Tuwa" during prayer time.

Sura 5: 3 states that Muslims are forbidden to eat dead meat, blood or swine, or any meat "Involved by Allah" So as it is, any of the messengers who report a command from Allah, all Muslims must follow. Nothing like the Blind, leading the Blind. Sura 4: 80 states, he who obeys the messenger, "Obeys Allah" How convenient.

In the Bible, Matthew 15: 14 states, they be Blind leaders of the Blind, and if the Blind lead the Blind, both shall fall into the ditch.

Sura 5: 45 states, Ordain equal for equal, life for life, eye for eye, nose for nose, ear for ear. This must be carried out by Muslims, but this does not involve inheritance, marriage or any command that Allah gives through his messengers, how convenient.

Sura 4: 150, 151, and 152 states, those who deny Allah, "and" his messenger and separate between Allah and his messenger, are not believers, Muslims are to make "No Distension" between "any" of the Messengers.

Sura 32: 23 states, "We" gave the book, " the bible and / or Torah" to Moses, and "we" made it a guide to the Children of Israel, Notice that this is given ONLY to the Jews of Israel or Christians, and leaves out any other religion.
Again in Sura 40: 53 "we" gave Moses the "guidance" and 'we' gave the book, (bible) in hesitance to the children of Israel. It can be easily believed that the Muslims have a very hard time trying to explain the children of Israel text given.

Moreover, Sura 87: 18 and 19 states, Books of the "earliest revelations" the books of Abraham and Moses, "thousands of years before Islam" this can be ONLY the OLD Testament Bible before Jesus was born to the Christians.
But then, Muslims don't understand the difference between Orthodox Jews and Christians. So they are at war to all of them who do not accept Allah.

It is nice to know that Sura 99: 2 reports the Earth s a "She" but then, Sura 16: 92 states "Be not like a Women" Muslim men cannot like females for any reason but to use them in a disregarding way for their purposes.

Anthropologist have proven that cannibalism has occurred in all parts of the world, it is interesting to find that the Qur'an brings up several times "Not to kill your children" it must have been a known fact that Muslims had a big problem with " either cannibalism or human sacrifice" or just pure hate for children.

Sura 6: 151 states, Kill Not your children on a plea of want.
Sura 17: 31 states, Kill Not your children for fear of want.
Sura 60: 12 states, take an oath of fealty, that they will Not Kill their children.

Do Muslims drink wine? See Sura 2: 219, states, concerning wine and gambling, "in them is great sin."

Sura 16: 67 states, from the fruit of the date, palm and the vine, you get out "Strong Drink"

Sura 47: 15 states, the description of the garden which the righteous "believers" are promised, in it are rivers of water installing, " unknown what installing is" (could mean stagnate.) Rivers of milk of which the taste never changes, "RIVERS OF WINE" A joy to those who drink, Allah must be confused again, if drinking wine is a sin in Sura 2: 219, then why is WINE available in the garden to the so called believers.

Sura 2: 140 states, do you say Abraham "Ishmael" Isaac and Jacob were Jews or Christians. Again Allah and his Muslims don't know the difference between an Orthodox Jew and a Christian, when you read this Qur'an scripture.

Sura 5: 12 states, Allah did afore time, "take a covenant" from the Children of Israel, given ONLY to the Children of Promise, and appointed twelve chieftains among them,

well this is interesting, here they admit that the Islam religion is with out the Promise of the Covenant, and simply stolen the covenant from the Israel people, now how do you think that can happen. Actually, if God gave the Covenant to Israel, then this would prove with out doubt, " Allah is Satan," and simply a false god for Islam, or Ishmael.

Sura 5: 14 states,, from those also, who call themselves " Christians" we did take a covenant "Their Promise" and we stirred up enmity and hatred between them.

This goes along with Sura 3: 28 which states, "Let not the believers take for friends or helpers unbelievers rather than believers. If any do that they shall have no relation left with Allah except by way of precaution. That you may guard yourselves from them. But Allah cautions you to far himself. For the final goal is to Allah.

Sura 17: 104 states, we said to the children of Israel, "Live securely in the land of Promise" Obviously Israel is the Land of Promise from God the Father. From this statement, Muslims know that Israel the Land of Promise from reading the Bible.

Sura 17: 111 states, Allah who begets no son, and has no partner in "his" dominion, this is different then Sura 16: 102, which states, the Holy Spirit has brought the revelation from the Lord of Truth. Obviously, Muslims must be very confused if they read this, as to who the Holy Spirit is, and what the Revelation would be.

Sura 10: 68 states, "they say" nonbelievers, Allah hath begotten a son, glory be to him, he is self sufficient, but if that being the case, then why use a messenger?

It looks to me Muslims think that we are calling God the Father "Allah" which is the biggest joke Muslims could think up ..

Sura 39: 53 states, Allah forgives "all sins" now see Sura 63: 6 states, it is "Equal" to them whether thou pray "asking" for their forgiveness or not, "ALLAH WILL NOT FORGIVE".

Sura 67: 11 states, "They will then confess their sins" but far from Allah's mercy are the companions of the blazing fire.

Mark 3: 28 in the Bible, Jesus said, "to His Children" ALL SINS shall be forgiven you. Luke 6: 37 states, to His Children, Forgive and you shall be forgiven.

Sura 75: 9 states, and the sun and moon are joined together.
Now see Sura 36: 40, states, It is NOT permitted to the Sun to catch up the Moon.

Sura 60: 4 states, there is for you an"excellent example" to follow in Abraham and those with him, they said to their people, we are clear of you and whatever you worship besides Allah, we have rejected you, and there has arisen between us and you enmity and hatred forever, unless you believe in Allah and him alone.

The Qur'an explains that this enmity and hatred is pointed to Jews and Christians and is known as their "Holy War" JIHAD, until they believe they have taken over the world for Allah.

Sura 61: 4 states, "Truly Allah loves those who FIGHT IN HIS NAME.
Sura 20: 71 and Sura 26: 49, that Pharaoh had tortured the Children of ISRAEL, thousands of years before Mohammad, Pharaoh was a worshiper of many false gods, and of them being one, called Allah, "the Moon god" Of which Mohammand adopted in his religion, and is carried by the Islamic faith.
From one end of the Qur'an to the other you can find where Allah has ordered killings of the Christians and Jews, or any people that will not worship Allah known as the unbelievers, see Sura 1: 191, states, KILL THEM where you find them.
Also Sura 5: 23, Assault them.
Sura 8: 65 States, O Prophet, rouse the believers to the FIGHT.
Sura 2: 216 state, Allah's command, "Fighting is prescribed upon you.
Sura 4: 75 and 76 state, and why should you NOT FIGHT in the cause of Allah.
Sura 4: 84 states, O you who believe, fight the unbelievers who are near to you and let them find harshness in you.

Sura 16: 110 states, those who strive and fight for the faith.
Sura 47: 4 states, when you meet the unbelievers "in fight" smite at their necks.
He, Allah, lets you fight in order to test you.

Sura 4: 91 states, Seize them and SLAY them wherever you get them.

Sura 4: 101 states, The unbelievers are unto you open enemies.

Sura 4: 59, 80, and Sura 24: 54, and 56 state, He who Obeys the Messenger, Obeys Allah.

Sura 42: 15 states, "Messengers make revelations with Allah's permission"

Sura 54: 40 states, "We" have indeed made the Qur'an easy to understand and remember. And Sura 43: 29 states, the messenger will make things clear.

That would be easy, if Muslims remember that all they have to remember is to KILL any one who will not believe in Allah, and worship the false god, who has to be Satan.

There is, NO OTHER RELIGION known on earth, that has "Orders from their god" to KILL and make it good to destroy other people in the name of a false god, like the Islamic religion. (THIS IS TRULY AN EVIL RELIGION)

Sura 27: 54, 55, and 56 states, We also sent Lot "as a messenger" Behold he said to his people, "Do you do what is indecent though you see it's iniquity?" Would you really approach men in your lusts rather then women? No, you are a people grossly ignorant. This message is clearly talking about the homosexual people in the Muslim community.

Sura 33: 59 through 61 explains women with their dressing, states, O prophet, tell the wives and daughters, and the believing women, when out doors, they should be known as such and not molested.

These verses in Sura 33: 59 to 61 is commanding the women to cover from head to foot, in order that a man will not get the idea to molest them.

Sura 33: 60 states, that those who do not believe, are hypocrites with a diseased heart who stir up sedition "resistance" which stir up anger in men to be cast out.

Sura 33: 61 states, that they "females" will have a curse on them, and wherever they are found, they shall e seized and slain, "killed" The Muslim men have such a curse on women, that Allah commands Muslim men not to be like a women, Sura 16: 92 states, be not like a women, who breaks into untwisted strands the yard she had spun.

Sura 34: 40 states, on the day he will gather them all together, and say to the angel, "Was it you that these men used to worship? They will say no, but they worshiped the Jinns " meaning Women" Most of them believed them.

Sura 51: 56 states, I have only created "Jinns and men" That they many serve me. It is clear that Jinns are women, who was created by the false god Allah in the Qur'an.

Sura 18: 50 states, Behold! "We" said to the angels, Prostrate to Adam, they prostrated except Lblis. "He was not one of the Jinns" And he broke the command of his Lord, will you then take him and his progeny "children" as the protectors rather than me? And they are enemies to you, evil would be the exchange for the wrong doers.

In the Qur'an, it is talking abut "Lblis" who is Satan, as a "he" as one of the Jinns, which in Sura 51: 56 states, Allah states that he has created ONLY JINNS and MEN, and Sura 7: 38 and 179 had made hell for Jinns and men. It must be that women and devils are one and the same. Additionally the Qur'an states in Sura 16: 92 "Be not like a women" Who breaks into untwisted stands after it becomes strong. "Using your oaths to deceive on another".

Sura 6: 128 states in part, on the day when he will gather them all together, and say, O you assembly of "JINNS" much toll you take of men.

As you can see by reading the facts and establishing the verses of this book, the "EVIL" of the Qur'an can be seen by any one not involved with Islam, and under the curse of Satan.

Knowing this, that JESUS CHRIST, the Lord and Savior of the Universe, for all believing Christians, is the ONLY Human who was sent by God the Father, His ONLY Begotten Son, who has "Split Time" at his Crucifixion on the Cross, shedding His Blood for the Payment of all sin in the world for those who believe on Him.

It is absolutely true and with out any doubt, Islamic "Fundamentalists" portray a heart of Islam. Muslims worship their cultural, intolerant, militant and world imperialistic religion of the "SWORD" of SATAN.

Evidence found in the Qur'an, or history that occurs every day engaged in a "WAR AGAINST TERRORISM" And our enemies are the Muslim Fundamentalist, but MOST of ALL, A war against THE CHIEF ANTICHRIST HIMSELF, THE ONE AND ONLY SATAN.

Now that I've gone through the Qur'an and established many different facts and fallacies, the burden of proof for Muhammad's call or any Muslim who wants to follow such religion because he is told to and not because he has a desire to, the burden of proof is upon the Muslims, And as we look at examining the arguments given by Muslims to see if in fact they hold up under careful scientific scrutiny.

We must state at the outset of this book is not to offend devout Muslims, we are not trying to hurt their feelings or embarrass them in any way, but to bring reality and truth to them in a way that will change their life for the better in turning from false doctrines and living a life of Truth in what is known as the True of God through the Bible, and no other.

Now to give you some history about the Islamic Religion and what they believe, Muslims take personal offense at any criticism of their religious beliefs, they find it very difficult to understand that "Freedom of Religion" In the West means that people are free to criticize Islam as well as any other religion.

Of course Muslims who live in the Eastern Nations will guard against any criticism of the Qur'an or Muhammad, and is looked upon as a Criminal Offense and Punishable by Death.

Since Muslims evidently have no problem what so ever in openly criticize other religions, why should they have a problem with those who for good and sufficient reasons criticize Islam or the Qur'an ?, after all, They are told by their messengers, to hunt and kill pagans that will not bend to their god Allah.

The meaning of Islam is not very hard to figure out, If you read Genesis 16: 11 in the Bible , God sent His Angel to Hagar, to tell her that she will bear a son, and his name shall be Ishmael, because God had heard of her affliction between Abram's first wife Sarai, and his name will dwell in the presence of all his brethren, (which is Islam today)
the Name Ishmael basically stands for a warrior who is fighting, even though it will be against the impossible odds.

Most interesting, the English word "Assassin" is actually an Arabic word, it comes from the Latin word assassins which is taken from the Arabic word hashshashin. This word means "smokers of hashish" or weed, and was used as a stimulant to get themselves into a religious frenzy before killing their enemies or pagans.

The assassins came into the European vocabulary through the Muslims who believed that Allah has called them to kill people as a sacred duty.

The Assassins terrorized the Middle East from the eleventh to the thirteenth century and even made the Western explorer Marco Polo fear for his life. This terrorism continues on today and it will not stop until Allah says it will stop, and h e isn't . talking.

The Quraysh tribe saw to it that there was an idol for every religion at the pagan temple called the KABAH. The word Kabah is Arabic for "CUBE" And refers to the square stone temple in Mecca where the idols were worshiped, the temple contained a virtual smorgasbord of deities with something for everyone.

More then 360 gods were represented at the Kabah and a new one could be added if some stranger came in to town and wanted to worship his own god in addition to the ones that were there.

The trade routes and rich caravans formed the cultural link between Africa, the Middle East, as well as the East and West. It is no surprise to find stories in the Qur'an that trace back to Egypt, Babylon, Persia, India and Greece.

In the Encyclopedia Britannica, the financial base of the Quraysh tribe depended on the caravans who came through Mecca for pagans to worship their particular idol at the Kabah.

John 17: 3 in the Christian Bible, it states for the Children of God, life is eternal, that they might know thee the Only True God, and Jesus Christ, whom thou has sent.

But for Muslims, Allah is unknowable, he is so transcendent, so exalted, that no man ever can personally know Allah.

God the Father of the Bible is spoken of as a personal being with intellect, emotion, and will. This is opposite to Allah, who is not to be understood as a person, this would lower Allah to the level of man.

To the Muslims, the idea that Allah is a person or a spirit is blasphemous because this would demean the exalted One. But the concept that "God is Spirit" is one of the cornerstones of the Biblical nature of God as taught by Jesus Himself, see John 4: 24 states, God is Spirit, and they that worship Him, Must Worship Him in Spirit and in Truth.

In the Bible, it states in Titus 1: 2 God cannot Lie, we are also told in Hebrews 6: 18 God can never act in a way that would contradict His Divine nature, and 2 Timothy 2: 13 , God cannot deny Himself, Although we serve a God of All knowing and All knowledge, His choice is to be Supreme, and it shows.
However, Allah on the other hand, can do "Anything, anytime, anyplace, with no limitations holding him, this is the reason he ask's his messengers to act out, and to give commands, moreover, Allah puts Jesus in charge (so to speak) to bring back the dead and heal the sick. How ridiculous is that for Allah, a god who needs NO help, as described.

Looking into history, it was impossible for the Bible to speak of "Allah as God," because until the Seventh century when Muhammad made Allah in his only god, Allah was the name of a pagan deity, Since the Bible was completed long before Muhammad was born, how could it speak of a post Muhammad or Allah?.
It's not possible to find the name Allah in the Scriptures of the bible, up until the time of Muhammad, Allah was simply one pagan god among many, his name is the name for the moon god as worship in Arabia.

Some may say that the name Allah was found in the biblical work "allelujah", being "alle" in the first part of the word was actually

"Allah" . But that Hebrew word allelujah is not a compound Hebrew word, Or not made up of two words, it is one single Hebrew word which means "praise to Yahweh". Also the name of God is in the last part of the word, "jah" which has reference to Yahweh or Jehovah. So Allah simply cannot be found in that word.

Also some may say,, when Jesus was on the Cross and He cried out "Eli, Eli ", He was actually saying "Allah,,, Allah". But this is not true either, the Greek New Testament at this point give us the Aramaic, not the Arabic translation of a portion of Psalm 22: 1, Jesus was saying, "My God, My God." Why hast thou forsaken me?. And the reason He said, why hast thou forsaken me, is because God the Father could not look on the Sin Jesus was washing away with His Own personal Blood. And God the Father just turned away from the Sin being taken away at that point of time, and Jesus knew that was happening that very moment.

There are those who may think that Allah is just another name for God, living in the West as well in the East, this is due to their ignorance of the differences between the Allah of the Qur'an and the God of the Bible, and also due to the propaganda Muslims use to try converting Westerners to Islam.

It is easy to find that Muhammad was born in 570 A.D. in Mecca to Abdullah and Aminah, he was born into the Quraysh tribe, which was in control of the city of Mecca and acted as the custodian of the Kabah and of the worship centered around it. Muhammad was sent to live with his grandparents because his father and mother died when Muhammad was a child. It is interesting to know that Muhammad grandparents and relatives lived and died pagans and never embraced Muhammad as a prophet nor did they accept Islam.

According to early Muslim Story telling, the young pagan Muhammad experienced miraculous visions he liked telling others, Muhammad had made claim that a heavenly being had split open his stomach, stirred his insides around, and then sewed him back up. Muhammad himself later refers to this story in Sura 94: 1 which states, Have "we" not expanded thee they breast?

Many Middle East scholars have felt that these early religious episodes may have been the result of some kind of mental problem or the medical problem of epilepsy.

Early Muslim tradition records the fact that when Muhammad was about to receive a revelation from Allah, he would often fall down on the ground, his body would begin to jerk, his eyes would roll backward, and he would perspire profusely, they would often cover him with a blanket during such episodes.

Muhammad would then claim that while he was in such a trance like state, he would receive divine visitations after the trance, and he would rise and proclaim what had been handed down to him..

Keep in mind, that in the Arab culture of Muhammad's day, epileptic seizures were interpreted as a religious sign of either demonic possession or divine visitation. Mohammad initially considered both options as possible interpretations of his experience. At first he worried about the possibility that he was demon possessed, this led him to attempt to commit suicide, but his wife was able to stop him from committing suicide by persuading him that he was such a good man that he could not possibly be demon possessed.

At age 40, Muhammad experienced once again a "visitation" As a result of his experience, he claimed Allah had called him to be a prophet and an apostle. It should be pointed out, that in the Arabian religion, it is not a tradition to being a prophet or apostle. The term Prophet was used in the hope that the Jews would accept

Muhammad as the next prophet, while the term apostle, was likewise used in the hope that the Christians would acknowledge him as the next apostle.

There are several alternative versions of this action by Muhammad in the Qur'an.

The Qur'an gives four conflicting accounts of this original call to be a prophet, either one of these four accounts are true and the others are false, or they are all false, they cannot all be true.
The Qur'an described Muhammad's initial call to be a prophet and apostle on four different occasions,
Sura 63: 2 to 18 and Sura 81: 19 to 24 states that Allah personally appeared to Muhammad in the form of a man and that Muhammad saw and heard him. It states in part, For he appeared (in stately form), then he approached and came closer, and was at a distance of but two bow-lengths or even nearer. For indeed he say him at a second descent, for truly did he see, of the signs of his Lord, the Greatest. Also Sura 81: 23 states, and without doubt he say him in the clear horizon.

But now, this claim is abandoned, as we see in Sura 16: 102 and Sura 26: 192 to 194 that Muhammad's call was issued by "the Holy Spirit".
Since Muhammad does not really discuss who or what this "Holy Spirit" is, This is also later abandoned, the third account of his original call is given in Sura 15: 8 where we are told that "the Angels" were the ones who came down to Muhammad and announced that Allah called him to be a prophet.
But even this account is later amended in Sura 2: 97, so that it is only the angel Gabriel who issues the call to Muhammad and hands down the Qur'an to him.
However, most Muslims and non-Muslims have heard that Muhammad assumed he was appropriately called to be the next great prophet in line.

Muhammad experienced other visions in which he felt that he had been told not to kill himself because he was truly called by God, yet even after this experience, he still became depressed and filled with doubt. His wife did convince him to become a prophet and with her encouragement he began preaching to his family, where his first converts of sorts, Soon his message became public, and he became a subject to abuse and ridicule.

At one point, the hostility against Muhammad was such that people in Mecca laid siege to the section of the city where Muhammad lived, he then faced a very difficult situation, it does state the oppression given to him,, see Sura 53: 23 which states, These are nothings but names which you have devised, you and your fathers, For which Allah has sent down NO Authority (what so ever) they follow nothing but, conjecture and what the souls desire, Even though there has already come to them guidance from their lord.

Muhammad's death is some what a mystery, he died in 632 A.D. There is some who have said that he was poisoned by a Jewish woman whose relatives were murdered in one of Muhammad's hate programs against Jews, Although Muhammad had no premonition of his own death, he made no arrangements for a successor,, neither did he gather or put together his various revelations into what is now known as the Qur'an.

The Birth of Jesus Christ was miraculous in that He was conceived by the Holy Spirit in the womb of the Virgin Mary.

The Qur'na and orthodox Islam fully accept the virgin birth of Jesus, it is only in modern times that we find some small heretical Muslim groups who deny and ridicule the doctrine of the virgin birth of Jesus, they do this out of reaction to the fact that there was nothing miraculous or supernatural about the birth of Muhammad

.. He was the natural product of the sexual union of his father and mother.

According to the Bible, Jesus Christ lived a perfect and sinless life, see 2 Corinthians 5: 21, when His enemies came to accuse Jesus before Pilate and Herod, they had to invent charges because no one could find anything against Him.

But when we turn to the life of Muhammad, we find that he was a normal human being engaged in the same sins which afflict all of us, he lied, he cheated, he lusted, he killed, he failed to keep his word, and on and on, He was neither perfect or sinless, but evil as evil can be.

If you ask any Muslim, they will of course say he sinned not, So just ask them to show in the Qur'an where Muhammad was sinless. Then some may say, Show where he sinned.

So I go to Sura 18: 110 and elsewhere, Muhammad is commanded by Allah, (Say, I am but a man like yourselves)
and see Sura 40: 55 where Allah told Muhammad to repent of his sins, ask forgiveness of your fault.

During Jesus life on earth, He did many great and mighty miracles, He healed the sick, raised the dead, Cast out demons, and even ruled the wind and the waves. But according to the Qur'an in many places, such as Sura 17: 91 to 95, Muhammad never performed a single miracle.

According to the Bible, Jesus preached the LOVE of GOD and was the greatest example of that Love, John 3: 16 states it exactly true, God so Loved the World, that He gave His Only begotten Son, that who so ever believes in Him should not perish but have eternal life.

In contrast, we do not have any record in the Qur'an of Muhammad ever preaching the Love of God. As a matter of fact, neither God's love for man nor man's love for God plays any significant role in the preaching of Muhammad, but you will find loads of Hate and killing.

Jesus is our intercessor and advocate in heaven, the only mediator between God and man see 1 Timothy 2: 5, But Muhammad is not an intercessor, in fact, the Qur'an states that there is no intercessor or savior, See Sura 6: 51, and 70 and Sura 10: 3 (you have to save yourself)

Devout Muslims believe that the rituals and doctrines of Islam comes from heaven and cannot have earthly sources, moreover, every ritual and belief in Islam can be traced back to pre-Islamic Arabian culture.
Muhammad did not preach any thing new, everything he said had been believed and practiced in Arabia long before he was ever born, even the idea of "only one God" was borrowed from the Jews and the Christians. This fact casts to the ground the Muslim claim that Islam was revealed from heaven, since its rituals, beliefs and even the Qur'an itself can be fully explained in terms of pre-Islamic sources in Arabian culture, this means that the religion of Islam is totally false.

When the facts point out wicked things that the Qur'an teaches, the Muslims will say, If your right, then the Bible is also wicked and you must reject the bible as well, because the bible has facts that point to wicked facts.

The problem is that prophethood is not the same in the Qur'an as in the bible, the bible does teach that prophets do sin like anyone else, The Big difference is that the bible states clearly that there is No private interpretation of man recorded in Scriptures, and ALL Scripture comes from God Himself, see 2 Peter 1: 21 (For the prophecy came not in Old Time by the will of man, but holy men of God spoke as they were moved by the Holy Spirit).

Also 2 Tim. 3: 16 ALL Scripture is given by inspiration of God, and is profitable for doctrine, for reproof, for correction, for instruction in righteousness.

This alone is fact that God has wrote our Bible for His Believers to follow.
The Qur'an is full of killing and hate for any one who will not believe in their false god.

Muslims will often make claim that Allah and the Christians or the Jewish God are one in the same, because there descended from Abraham, where actually, we all are descended from ADAM and from there, we are descendants from his offspring, Seth and Cain, and from there Abraham's two sons, Isaac and Ishmael, and from there, the Christians are from Isaac and the others are from Ishmael.

Just as Jesus explains His generation back to David and then Abraham and Isaac in Matt. 1: 1.

I am sure there is a great deal more that could be said, but if the facts are not evident my now, they will never be. Mohammad is a fake and deceiver, and his followers will be as it says in the Bible, a Wild man and against every man, just as Satan wants for the children of Jesus.

For where there is an action, There will be a re-action, and where there is good, there will be evil, Where there is Salvation, there will be damnation. When you have one, you will have the other. So take your pick.

The End.

Printed in Great Britain
by Amazon

83505987R00041